Small Business Trendsetters

Online Strategies For Your Local Business

John Deck
Rebecca Holman
Dave Birchall
Chet Bruce
Daren Baysinger
Clarence Close
Rob Mullins
Kimberlee Canducci
Virginia Drew
Anthony Smith

DMR Publishing

Sacramento, California

Printed Edition Published By:
DMR Publishing, part of Direct Market Results
Sacramento, California
www.DMRpublishing.com

Book Layout © 2014 BookDesignTemplates.com

Small Business Trendsetters. – 2nd ed.
ISBN 978-0-9861833-2-4

CONTENTS

AdWords (PPC) For Lead Generation 1

John R. Deck.................................. 4

Insights From the Inside... What Works For My Business
Clients Today.. 5

Rebecca Holman 7

If They Can't See You - They Can't Find You!.................... 9

Dave Birchall 13

Give the Consumer What They Want 15

Chet Bruce 18

Video Provides Small Business Owners The Biggest Bang
For Their Marketing Buck..............................19

Daren Baysinger 21

Using Videos to Grab Attention..........................23

Clarence Close 27

Facebook Goldmine How To Stake Your Claim..................29

Rob Mullins 33

The Complete Marketing System That Can Skyrocket Your
Revenue and Crush The Competition in 12 Months 35

Kimberlee Canducci.......................................38

Is Your Website a Customer Magnet...Or An Arid
Wasteland?..39

Virginia Drew 42

Your Online Reputation – From Being Found "Online" To
Being Profitable "Offline" 43

Anthony Smith................................47

CHAPTER ONE

AdWords (PPC) For Lead Generation

By John R. Deck

In many markets, PPC (pay per click) is one of the most cost effective source for new business. For a couple of my clients, the only source that beats PPC on cost is client referrals (which are almost free).

Probably one of the quickest ways for a local business to start generating additional customers or client leads is with Google's AdWords. These are ads that show up in Google's search results. They can generally be seen at the top of the search results and along the right side. Many businesses that have tried Google AdWords in the past have gotten poor results even when Google, or 'big G', itself ran the campaign.

AdWords is not for all businesses. However, when it works, it can be one of the lowest-cost sources for new customers. Frankly, for a number of my clients, the only cheaper source of new clients is referrals from existing customers.

So what do you need to do to have a successful starter AdWords campaign?

Start by targeting only one, maybe two, money keywords. What are money keywords? These are keywords that BUY-ERS use to find your businesses. Here are some examples.

'roof repair Austin'
'24 hour plumber Austin'
'carpet cleaning Austin'

In the examples above Austin is used for the target city. You would use the city where your business is located. If you live in Fresno, California and do carpet cleaning, then you would target 'carpet cleaning Fresno' (without the single quotes).

Business owners are often told they need ten, twenty or even a hundred keywords to start their campaign. This is not true. People giving this advice do not know local businesses, and are just hoping they might hit the best keyword to target. The problem is the local business owner pays while these 'experts' try to figure the right keyword. BTW, that applies to big G run campaigns as well. Their representatives are well trained but few really know how to work with local businesses.

Limit the geographic reach of the campaign. A local business is, well, local. People do most of their shopping within five to twenty miles from home. They will only drive further if they cannot find what they need within their immediate area. So set the geographic area of the campaign to no more than 30 to 50 miles. Only go further out if you have multiple locations, or know that you can pull customers beyond 50 miles from your business. Do not pay for AdWords clicks from people who will not drive to your store location. If the campaign is working then extend it out to your local metro area. Only testing will tell if that will bring enough additional business to cover the increase in cost.

The largest percentage of buyers will search for your product or service during business hours. Yes, there are buyers searching during off hours. However, searches during off hours are most likely information searches. Now, information searches are valuable as well. However, the goal here is to get new buyers as quickly and at the lowest possible cost. So set the time your AdWords ad runs to your business hours and the days the business is open. After the campaign is successfully generating new customers, then expand the hours the ad runs. In some cases running the campaign in off hours makes a difference. I have seen campaigns that 90% of the business comes during business hours. While other campaigns, running the ad during off hours was well worth it.

To Summarize:

Start with one, maybe two money keywords. Limit the geographic reach of the AdWords campaign. Have the ads only run during business hours when someone is available to answer the phone.

One last suggestion: Answer the phone! Do not let phone calls roll into voice mail. This can make or break a campaign. If someone is ready to buy and their call is not answered, they will almost always call another business.

John R. Deck

Sacramento, California
http://www.DirectMarketResults.com
info@DirectMarketResults.com

CHAPTER TWO

Insights From the Inside...
What Works For My Business
Clients Today

By Rebecca Holman

As an online marketer now for a few years, I have tried many and varied tactics to help my clients get front and center in their marketplace. Some clients are local, and some clients needed a broader, international reach.

After using, PPC, Video Marketing, FaceBook Fanpages and FaceBook ads and Clickable Ads, I feel more and more strongly that Press Releases give the best bang for my clients' buck. With a senior editor at Newswire.net helping me get it posted, I do have an unfair advantage over other people. Having used a senior editor on several projects, I feel that we have way better results for the money spent.

The reason that Press Releases are so powerful is that the traffic is already there. I don't have to focus on driving traffic to the article written. Doing some simple keyword research and using those terms for SEO can help get the article found much easier, but it is not really necessary, if the topic is timely and written in an engaging and news worthy fashion.

I have used Press Releases and been able to track the results in responses we have received. One such example is a Kickstarter campaign – one that had sat idle for a number of days. The Press Release added new life to the campaign and we added many more contributors and dollars to the Kickstarter project that otherwise would not have even found page one.

Press Release articles I have written for my clients have had thousands of views, and those views translated into new customers spending money in the client's business. If I had paid PPC prices for this client, who is in a medical niche, I would have had to pay hundreds if not thousands of dollars for the same results.

I use PPC for this particular local offline client now so I know firsthand how little return we get for the hundreds we spend each month. It is for this powerful reason I now urge clients to spend the money on a Press Release for their business, whether they are local, national or internationally based.

Rebecca Holman

http://missoulaseoguru.com

CHAPTER THREE

If They Can't See You - They Can't Find You!

By Dave Birchall

If you have to compete with the Big Boys in your sector, businesses who have Millions of £/$/Yen to throw at marketing, then getting your fair share of the cake can be hard. You wonder sometimes if it is worth all the money you spend with agencies and on traditional advertising.

The 21st Century has compounded the marketing problem for the smaller firms. We understood to some extent about Newspapers, Magazines, Bill-boards, TV and Radio, even if we could not afford them too often or even at all.

Now the Internet has opened up so much more that it can be mind-blowing just to consider how you should market your products or services to win paying customers.

Don't worry – The Playing Field is About to Be Leveled!

The fact is that the Internet gives you the same opportunities as it does the Big International Corporations, but if you play your cards right it will always favour you over the Large Corps.

Why? – Because search engines like Google, Bing and Yahoo favour LOCAL over International, because their statistics tell them that most searches on the Internet (over 85%) are for Local Suppliers of goods or services. And that is where you can grab the leading edge if you know what to do.

How Do You Do That?

Well, the key is to understanding what your customer is looking for and where they are looking to find it. That might sound silly, but it's a fact! And it does not matter whether you are selling pizzas or armchairs, health and professional services, general services or trade skills, – **be where they are looking.**

How Can You Do That?

Text/SMS

Website

Email & Auto Responders

On Line Marketing & Sales

Mobile Website

QR Codes

Landing Pages

Directories and Social Media

Be aware of change!

The computer is no longer the preferred tool to search the Internet; more people now use their mobile phones (cell phones) to find what they are looking for. *Can they find you with their phone?*

They are searching – Google, Bing, Yahoo, Facebook, YouTube, Pinterest, LinkedIn, Twitter, Craigslist, Backpage, GumTree, QR Codes, Amazon, iTunes and so on…

Yes I know, seeing all that does not make it look as easy as I say it is, huh? Well, like everything else you have to start somewhere and I usually point my clients towards *YouTube and Pinterest* first.

Why? Because they are similar and once you have set them up you can look at the others with more confidence.

A good video on YouTube is inexpensive and can paint a thousand words in a short space of time. The same is true with Pinterest. If you add a "Call To Action" with a button or QR Code to your video and photographs, then you can get mobile phones clicking to call you.

Now, I guess you think, "It's Not That Easy". Well, you're right, but it's *not as difficult as you think it is, nor is it as expensive as much of the traditional advertising you have been used to.*

We understand how the Internet works and can get you on the right path *at a pace you can cope with online and offline.* You are the experts at knowing your customers – we are the experts at knowing how to reach them and together we'll make a great team.

Want to know more about growing your Local Market?

Then we can help –

Contact Dave Birchall at +44 1 5395 31338 or http://helpmysmallbusiness.co.uk

– You'll be surprised at how quickly you can have our skills at your fingertips!

Dave Birchall

http://helpmysmallbusiness.co.uk

Give the Consumer What They Want

By Chet Bruce

One hundred business owners will see this article today. Of those, 50 will no longer be in business in five years. Only five will still be in business in ten years.

The five that will survive are the ones that "Transformed" and adapted to the modern market place using the results of published psychological research on consumers.

Let me be clear, this is about surviving the Transformation that consumers have made. It started in the early 90's and reached its culmination in the early years of the 21st Century.

The Internet, and how consumers use it, is the cause of the Transformation. In the Prospecting section of the Plan we talk about the right way to use the Internet and it has very little to do with the BS you hear about Internet Marketing on a daily basis.

Merchants, Professionals, Direct Service Representatives and Sales Managers must "Transform" if they are to survive the changes that have taken place in a consumers thinking in today's Market Place.

The Six Components must be considered when making your own "Transformation Plan".

1. Your Foundation
2. Prospecting
3. The Interview
4. The Proposal
5. The Close
6. Constant Follow Up

Today we are going to look at one of the most underused marketing functions on the Internet available to any merchant today, which falls under the 'Prospecting' component.

Classified Advertising

Online Classifieds are the most underused, high producing sites anywhere on the Net. The reason they are underused is because merchants do not know how to use them.

Let me give you a case study of just one case where a classified ad produced over $3000 for a client in less than a week after it was published.

My client was a Bankruptcy Attorney. He was faced with other services (usually not attorneys) advertising bankruptcies for $799. His normal average fee was $2400.

One day after his ad exposing the $799 services became active in USFreeads.com he received a phone call. The call came from a prospect living an hour away from his office.

After a 20-minute conversation, the prospect made an appointment for two days later.

That appointment took 30 minutes to close the deal.

Of course the reason that the ad converted had 100% to do with the fact that the ad was not the usual all text or picture with text that is usually used. The reason it converted was the fact that the ad appeared to have a video posted there.

Now of course, most Classified Sites do not allow video to be displayed or played from their sites.

Browse to this address to see a sample of what a dynamic page looks like on a classified site (The links are not active as this is not on Craigslist but on my own server. It is not intended to be available to the public and in no way competes with Craigslist. It is shown only as an example);

http://www.craigslist-video-ads.com/craigslist-inland-empire/

When a prospect clicks on the video play button they will be taken to your Landing Page where the video will play.

Some Classified Sites
Craigs List http://www.craigslist.org/
Back Page http://www.backpage.com/
Oodle http://www.oodle.com
Olx http://www.olx.com
EBay Classifieds http://www.ebayclassifieds.com
Domestic Sale http://www.domesticsale.com
Classified Ads http://www.classifiedads.com
US Free Ads http://www.usfreeads.com

Some have restrictions. Most are free. Not all will allow linked images. Read the Terms of Use before registering for use.

Chet Bruce

http://21stcenturytransformation.c4aba.us

CHAPTER FIVE

Video Provides Small Business Owners The Biggest Bang For Their Marketing Buck

By Daren Baysinger

Local business owners should consider using video to promote their business online for several very important reasons.

Video is growing faster than any other form of online marketing. Since purchasing YouTube several years ago, Google has included video more and more into search results for specific topics.

Simple but highly effective videos can be created quickly and easily. For those with little or no video creation experience using online video production software, such as Animoto, can provide a great starting point to learn the ins and outs of video creation.

Unlike many other local marketing tactics, video marketing is simple, cost-effective and can provide almost instant results. A properly structured video submission can get a small business on the first page of Google in as little as a few minutes.

A powerful method for using video includes promoting special offers in conjunction with local fairs or seasonal events. This will help get higher search engine rankings and generate maximum views.

The best site to upload your new marketing video to is YouTube. Creating an account is as easy as creating a Gmail account.

When using video to promote a business or service make sure:

- The video is 3-5 minutes long and includes a compelling offer, or call to action.

- The video title contains the key words that local consumers will most likely be searching for.

- The main website URL is included in the description of the video.

- And, the description is written to include other key words or terms related to whatever you are promoting.

Once the video is uploaded to YouTube, be sure to like and share the video with everyone you can think of. Videos that rank highest on YouTube also tend to have more views than other videos.

After you've mastered YouTube you can move on to promoting your video on other video hosting sites like Vimeo and Viddler. A simple search in Google for "Free Video Hosting Sites" will provide more than enough places to host your new marketing video.

Daren Baysinger

http:// DarenBaysinger.com

CHAPTER SIX

Using Videos to Grab Attention

By Clarence Close

If you want a simple tactic to use online to bring in more Customers, Clients, or Patients, consider the following:

If you are a local business and you are not using videos on Youtube to reach your Customers, Clients, or Patients, you are leaving good money on the table!

Look, I challenge you to go to Google and do a search for a topic.

Use these search phrases (without quotes) for example:

"Workers Comp Lawyer Pocatello"
or

"Dentist Tokyo"

or

"Kansas City Auto Repair"

or

"Boise Legal Nurse Consultant".

Go ahead and give it a try, I'll wait.

What do you see? Listing of businesses, some Google places listings, and a video.

What were your eyes attracted to first?

The video?

If you answered yes, then you are doing what the vast majority of searchers would do when they search for your product or service online.

The human eye, the mind is attracted to visual imagery. It is the way the mind works. As a species, we are looking for visual clues.

Now that you understand what attracts the eye, what is the next useful thing you see on the video listing? A phone number, right?

Did you also know that if someone is looking for a business, doing a Google search online, and they are getting down to specifics, for the most part, they are in need.

They may not watch the video. They will just pick up the phone and make the call.

If they do, you now have the opportunity to get them as a Customer, a Client, or a Patient, depending upon your goal and profession.

Now suppose they do watch the video.

Even better.

Now you get to address some of their concerns.

You get to speak to the reason they did the search on Google anyway.

Now they get to know you, like you, and trust you because you spoke directly to their needs.

It is a powerful way of getting an introduction, without being introduced.

At the end of your simple short video, you put a call to action.

A What?

A Call To Action. Just tell them what you want them to do.

Something like:

"Call Me at (Your Phone Number)"

or

"Come By and Get a Free (whatever you are offering)"

Or , and this is really good so you can see how effective is your video at bringing in customers tell them,

"Mention This Video and 'Get a Free (Something)'/'A 25% Discount On (a service or product)'."

Can you begin to see how this can work for you?

How it can pique their interest enough for them to actually contact your business?

Of course once they do make this contact, you need to close the deal.

But then that is what you do best, right? Now, how do you get the video on page one of the search results?

I'll leave that for another conversation, as it can be more technical than you really want to know.

You can see that a well-placed video:

1. Attracts the eye.
2. Can precipitate a phone call.
3. Can get your compelling message into their hearing.
4. Can then assist them in knowing what to do next, which is contact you for your expertise or offer.

In my experience, nothing works better than a well-placed video. Heck, if this book had a way to play a video, I would use it to tell you the exact same thing I wrote you above!

If you need any further assistance in making a video or assuring that it can be found by prospective Customers, Clients, or Patients searching for your product or service online:

Go To My Website at MarketingPartnerOnline.com

Email Me at clarence@marketingpartneronline.com

Call Me at (208) 238-0493.

"I am your Marketing Partner Online. How Can I Help You."

Clarence Close

http://marketingpartneronline.com/

CHAPTER SEVEN

Facebook Goldmine
How To Stake Your Claim

By Rob Mullins

All local business owners recognize the importance of being known in their community as a source of reliable goods and services. It's a fundamental need of any business. The question is – does your small business have enough consistent exposure to customers who are willing and able to make buying decisions? Is your business being found online and offline, today?

Most business owners have also figured out that their business needs to have some sort of presence in the world of Social Media. You don't have to look very far to find the latest study that shows ever increasing numbers of people are using the Internet to find local products and services. That's the good news. The bad news is, there are so many options to choose from - where do you start???

Here's a specific tactic you can begin using today to help your business presence. That tactic is optimizing your business Facebook Fan page.

There are a number of ways you can get the most exposure for your business with each and every post you place on your Facebook Fan page.

If you've been just adding random post to your business FB page, now is the time to take full advantage of each post. It won't take you much longer, but the ROI (return on investment) will be much higher.

There's one core principle that most business owners still have not embraced when working with their FB Fan page. That principle is "Relationship".

One of the most important priorities of your Facebook business strategy is attracting and converting new prospects who have visited your FB Fan page. You must go beyond just describing your business products and services and all the special prices you're running. Your opportunity is to add value to the people who visit your FB page and give them experiences that make them want to come back.

Below are some ideas for you to explore. We don't have time or space in this publication to go into detailed "how-to" explanations. For now, let's look at some opportunities;

- Promoted posts. These are posts that you pay Facebook to place in front of certain types of people

- Promotion within your post. You can make an offer and include a link to one of your external webpages.

- Memes. Those pictorial posts that have a short memorable saying or quote

- Multimedia. Studies have proven that photos and videos can improve the chances that people will stay longer on your FB page, which increases the likelihood of them making a business buying decision. Use lots of images and photographs of people. They can pull people in who have landed on your page and are just scanning.

- Link your Facebook Fan page to your Twitter account to maximize your business message exposure.

- Asking for customer feedback is a great way to not only find out what's of interest and importance to them, but also to help them feel more connected to you and your business. Remember, it's all about building a business relationship. Your personal engagement with those who leave comments to your posts is another very effective way to let people know you care and that you are a trusted and credible resource.

- Ask questions to provoke engagement. This could be something as fun and simple as, "What is your favorite movie in the last 2 months?"…or… "What's one word that best describes how you're feeling today?"

- Another area that you can explore to optimize your Facebook page will involve some business measurement and analysis.

Are you up for some fun math? To do this you'll need to keep track of some Facebook activity like;

- What's the right number of posts per day or per week?

- What's the best timing of posts? (early in the day, late in the day, or on certain days of the week)

As you can see there are some very easy and accessible actions you can take to help your business be found online.

Your business Facebook Fan page is a gold mine of opportunity that is just waiting for you.

Decide today, what one or two ideas you can work on and implement?

Take action today and your business will thank you.

If you would like to know more about how to take full advantage of Facebook marketing or need any assistance, please email me at robmullinsmarketing@gmail.com
All the best to you,

Rob Mullins

Garden Grove, California
http://chiropracticbusinessjournal.com

CHAPTER EIGHT

The Complete Marketing System That Can Skyrocket Your Revenue and Crush The Competition in 12 Months

By Kimberlee Canducci

What you're about to learn can lead to explosive growth in your business.

The number one reason why most businesses fail isn't because of a lack of capital. It's because sales don't come in fast enough to cover expenses. And in most cases, the business owner is so busy running the business he doesn't have the time (or the money) to invest in learning how to craft a compelling message or to keep up with the rapidly changing online media that can help him market cost-effectively.

By now you know that traditional methods of advertising just aren't as effective as they use to be. Maybe you've relied on the yellow pages, or Val Pak, or newspaper advertising and spent hundreds if not thousands of dollars for little or no results. Maybe you have a friend or college kid who's tried to use social media to bring in business. Maybe you've even put a video up on You Tube.

Three Essential Components Every Business Needs to Be Successful

The shift to online marketing and mobile technology has forever changed the landscape of business, but it's also leveled the playing field to allow small businesses to compete with larger companies with bigger budgets. But large or small, every business needs these three elements to survive, grow and thrive in today's marketplace.

Comprehensive Internet Marketing System

When Local Customers Search For What You Sell, Do They Find You?

Recent research shows that 90% of online commercial searches results in local offline purchases. And over 61% of all local searches result in a transaction. Marketing online isn't optional anymore – it's essential.

A well-designed Internet marketing presence will make your business findable in multiple places online – the places where consumers look when they're ready to buy. Social media, Youtube, blog posts, articles, press releases, online directories and review sites are all opportunities for consumers to find your compelling message.

A Strategic Messaging System

Having a website without traffic is like having the proverbial billboard in the desert. But it's not just about having people find your website. The bigger question is, what do they see when they find it? If they found your website, they probably saw your competitors' site too. Why should they choose you over them?

Before you decide where to spend your marketing budget, the first step is to have a strategic, compelling message that resonates with your prospects. This enables your company to build an effective marketing message that shows prospects you have the solution they're looking for. That means having messaging that is both important and relevant to your target market.

This is so important - having an effective strategic message is the critical difference between effective marketing and under-leveraged marketing.

A Systemized Marketing Process

Having an automated online marketing program that utilizes online videos, captures leads and delivers automatic follow-ups through email, text messaging, and direct-to-voicemail messages will drive online visibility for relevant searches. It also incorporates a company's online presence into their overall marketing program.

Most importantly, having a systemized marketing process ensures a consistent customer experience, streamlines lead generation and conversion, and creates efficiencies in your business.

To learn more and get free marketing resources to visit http://www.clientmarketingpower.com

Kimberlee Canducci

http://www.clientmarketingpower.com

CHAPTER NINE

Is Your Website a Customer Magnet...Or An Arid Wasteland?

By Virginia Drew

The business website is a basic tool that any business can use to get a constant flow of new customers in the door, or to keep the phones ringing. A lot of businesses have a website that looks gorgeous. The owner is proud to show it off to family and friends.

But that website is worthless to the business if either it doesn't attract any prospects or, once they get there they can't figure out what to do next and they leave.

An effective website is not difficult to design. Just keep in mind that it has one purpose. That is to attract prospects and get them to contact you, preferably by calling or walking in the door. If you want them to call, your phone number should be front and center on the page. If you want them to visit your store, your address should stand out.

I am always surprised at the number of business websites that force the visitor to search for the phone number (or any contact information at all). That is like a retail business with a tiny entrance door where no one can see it.

The next step is to attract prospects to your site. One free way to do this is through Search Engine Optimization (SEO). The term "SEO" just means making your site findable so when people search in Google for your business your website shows up at or near the top of the results. There is a bit of a science to it, but for most local businesses it is not that difficult because the competition has not yet caught on.

To understand why these methods of SEO work, you have to know that 95% of Google's income comes from AdWords advertising. In order to make money from AdWords they have to have a lot of people using their search engine. In order to do that, they need to provide the best possible results when someone searches.

So, good SEO just means convincing Google that your site is one of the best results when someone is searching for your products or services. This is done in 2 ways. You need to have certain things in place both on and off your website. What you do on your site is known as on-page SEO and what you do off your site is called off-page SEO

On-page SEO

To have good on-page SEO you must make it obvious to anyone visiting your site where you are located and what you do. The exact means to do this are beyond the scope of this article but, to summarize, there are several aspects to good on-page SEO.

You have to have your business name, address, and phone number appear several times in different locations throughout your site. You have to have a good title and well-written description for your pages, as well as a short but well-chosen list of keywords. You should also have some inside pages with relevant articles that link to your home page. The best platform is a WordPress blog.

Off-page SEO

For most local businesses it is not necessary to do a lot of off-page SEO. You should start with one or two things and only add more if you have to.

Social Bookmarking: There are sites that allow you to put a link to your site on their site. One type is a social bookmark. This would be done on a site such as Digg.com.

Backlinking from prestigious sites: This is like living in a nice neighborhood. If you get links from sites Google likes, it appears that those sites approve of your site and therefore Google will look more favorably on your site as well.

Creating your own network of high page rank sites. This is a very advanced method, but is very effective even in the more competitive markets. You can purchase sites with a high ranking and then link from them to your business site. There are also companies that maintain these sites from whom you can purchase links.

So, when you are trying to figure out how best to get customers from the internet, remember that one of your best online tools is your website. It is inexpensive to create, almost free to maintain and, if created and promoted properly, is an effective way to get new customers into any business. It is not that difficult, either, because most of the competition is doing everything wrong. This presents a great opportunity for any local business.

If you have any questions, feel free to send me an email at vldrew2@gmail.com

Virginia Drew

http://www.localexpertpublicity.com

Your Online Reputation – From Being Found "Online" To Being Profitable "Offline"

By Anthony Smith

Question...

What are people ALREADY saying about you and your business on the Web?

Are there glowing reviews? Negative feedback and slanderous comments? Or nothing at all? How about your competition – what's the state of their online reputation? Do you know how to find out?

The rise of social media sites like Facebook, YouTube, and Twitter as well as a wide variety of business review sites and tools like Google Reviews has meant that savvy business owners need to look beyond the content displayed on their website. You need to actively monitor what consumers, local competitors, and even disgruntled ex-employees are saying about you and your business across the Web.

Although glowing client feedback and reviews on third-party websites can significantly boost your online credibility – leading to more business – negative feedback can be VERY damaging. This is especially true when there are absolutely NO positive reviews or feedback to counteract the negative comments.

So today, more than ever, it's critical that you actively monitor and manage your online reputation.

And there are two ways to do this: proactively and reactively.

It should be obvious why I would recommend the former rather than the latter, but in case it isn't, here are the main reasons why...

Proactive Online Reputation Management (RECOM-MENDED!) allows you to:

1.   Create **controlled spaces** for clients to discuss your business on the Web (like via Facebook, Twitter, & YouTube).

2. Put **feedback loops** in place that compels your most satisfied customers to automatically post glowing reviews of your business in public forums and Google Reviews.

3. Systematically **create content for third-party sites** (articles, videos, expert interviews, press releases, etc.) that establishes your 'voice' as THE authority in your local market. **(Important: You don't need to create this content yourself; it's surprisingly affordable for local businesses to outsource content development of this type these days – let me give you a FREE QUOTE and prove it is very easy!)**

4. **And dominate the 'organic' Google search listings** with listings for your website, Facebook page, YouTube videos, positive client reviews, and more – making any negative feedback almost invisible among all the POSTIVE communication that surrounds your business.

While Reactive Online Reputation Management (not recommended) means you have to...

1. Try to have any negative feedback posted about your business resolved or **removed from the Web (DIFFICULT!)**

2. Take positive steps to **openly and honestly deal with the negative reviews** in a public forum.

3. **And begin proactively managing your online reputation** to essentially dilute and decrease the visibility of the negative feedback anyway.

Obviously, it makes more sense to proactively manage your online reputation. But if the negative feedback is already out there, then you'll need some help to do damage control as well.

If your competition begins proactively managing their online reputation while you continue to ignore this critical piece of online marketing, your business could be at serious risk of being pushed OUT OF VIEW in the search engine rankings...

... And playing catch-up 6 or 12 months down the road can be FIVE TIMES more costly than getting started today, while you have the first-mover advantage!

To start proactively managing your online reputation today, simply contact an online reputation specialist in your area who has the credibility of being a best-selling author on the topic, or guarantee you will find one by going directly to http://www.anthonydsmith.com for help. I, or a member of my team, will be waiting to meet you there.

Anthony Smith

http://www.anthonydsmith.com

NOTES: